THE HANG

Other Books by Taylor Mac Available from TCG

Gary: A Sequel to Titus Andronicus

THE HANG

Libretto by **TAYLOR MAC**

Music by **MATT RAY**

THEATRE COMMUNICATIONS GROUP
NEW YORK
2026

The Hang is published by Theatre Communications Group, Inc.,
520 Eighth Avenue, 20th Floor, Suite 2000, New York, NY 10018-4156

TCG books are exclusively distributed to the book trade by Consortium Book Sales and Distribution.

ISBN 978-1-63670-188-2 (paperback) / ISBN 978-1-63670-189-9 (ebook)

A catalog record for this book is available from the Library of Congress.

tcg

www.tcg.org
Follow us on Instagram @tcg_gram

Cover design, book design and composition by Lisa Govan
Cover art by Anastasia Durasova

First Edition, February 2026

"*The Hang* feels like a celebration of theater itself—a paean to collaboration and company, to rampant beauty and to the necessary balm of gathering together . . . a ritual of splendor and an exaltation of queerness."

—**LAURA COLLINS-HUGHES, *NEW YORK TIMES***

"I frickin' love *The Hang*."

—**VINSON CUNNINGHAM, *NEW YORKER***

"The most daring aspect of *The Hang* is also its most heartening: About a man's death from hemlock poisoning, it is unfailingly joyous and never takes itself too seriously. It is a radical declaration of queer frivolity in our severe age, and it restores my faith that there is still room for dangerous ideas and weird people in the New York theater."

—**ZACHARY STEWART, *THEATERMANIA***

"At a time when self-restraint and simple good taste can seem in desperately short supply, Mac continues to be that rare artist who proves that sometimes too much is exactly enough."

—**ELYSA GARDNER, *NEW YORK STAGE REVIEW***

"Beautiful, enveloping, and wild . . . a house party crossed with a New Orleans funeral procession married to a Radical Faerie bacchanal."

—**HELEN SHAW, *VULTURE***

"*The Hang* reminds us why we gather together with strangers in these dark rooms . . . We've come together for fellowship and communion, to bask in a creative space that transforms into a mythopoetic orgy of mourning and celebration and catharsis. As the chorus repeats: we're 'in it for the hang.'"

—**JERRY PORTWOOD, *THEATRELY***

The latest work from playwright Taylor Mac and composer Matt Ray takes us to ancient Athens on the eve of Socrates' death. Sentenced to die for "corrupting the youth," Socrates decides to spend his remaining hours doing what he loves: engaging in philosophical debate, singing, and dancing. And just, you know . . . *hanging out*. The result is a musical-theatrical riff on philosophical history, considering injustice, virtue, and prayer as an act of wondering. Along the way, Plato dutifully but inaccurately records events, reminding us that life's (and theater's) truest pleasures are the unwritable moments of joyous communion. *The Hang* is a joyfully queer fantasia that blends jazz and opera to reimagine the final hours of Socrates.

TAYLOR MAC is a MacArthur Fellow, a Pulitzer Prize finalist, a Tony nominee for Best Play, and the recipient of the International Ibsen Award. Selected works include: *Bark of Millions* (a fifty-five song—and counting—parade trance extravaganza for the living library of the deviant theme); *A 24-Decade History of Popular Music* (a twenty-four-hour performance-art concert about communities building themselves because they're torn apart); and *An American Dionysia* (four plays about the polarization of America: *Prosperous Fools*, *The Fre*, *Gary*, and *Hir*). The concert-doc, *Taylor Mac's 24-Decade History of Popular Music*, is currently streaming on HBO Max.

MATT RAY is a composer, arranger, theater maker, pianist, singer, songwriter, and music director living in New York. He is a fixture of New York's downtown cabaret and nightlife scene, having collaborated with luminaries such as Taylor Mac, Justin Vivian Bond, Bridget Everett, and Joey Arias. For his composition and music direction on his and Mac's jazz-based theater piece *The Hang* (HERE Arts Center, 2022), Matt received a 2023 Obie Award. The show also received four Drama Desk and two Drama League nominations, including a Drama Desk nomination for Matt Ray for Best Music. Other Ray and Mac collaborations include *The Lily's Revenge* (HERE Arts Center, 2009), *Bark of Millions* (Sydney Opera House, 2023), and *A 24-Decade History of Popular Music* (St. Ann's Warehouse, 2016). For his work on *24-Decade*, he and Mac shared the 2017 Kennedy Prize for Drama Inspired by American History.

Stay a little while longer.
There is still time to consider virtue.

—SOCRATES
(FROM PLATO'S *THE APOLOGY*)

THE HANG

PRODUCTION HISTORY

The Hang was commissioned, developed, and produced by the HERE Arts Center, with support from The Roy Cockrum Foundation, the MAP Fund, the New England Foundation for the Arts, the Mertz Gilmore Foundation, and the Andrew W. Mellon Foundation's National Playwright Residency Program. The world premiere was presented at the HERE Arts Center (Kristin Marting, Founding Artistic Director; Meredith Lynsey Schade, Producing Director), in New York City in January 2022. The production was directed by Niegel Smith. The scenic and costume design were by Machine Dazzle; the lighting design was by Kate McGee; the sound design was by Cricket S. Myers; the makeup design was by Anastasia Durasova; and the music and music direction were by Matt Ray. The choreography was by Chanon Judson; the dramaturg was Morgan Jenness; and the production stage manager was Patrick David Egan. The cast included Taylor Mac, Kenneth Ard, El Beh, Ryan Chittaphong, Kat Edmonson, Queen Esther, Wesley Garlington, Synead Cidney Nichols, and Trebien Pollard. The featured musicians were Matt Ray, Jonathan Beshay, Greg Glassman, J. Walter Hawkes, Jessica Lurie, Joel Mateo, Lisa Parrott, and Gary Wang.

CHARACTERS

SOCRATES (also plays Noël Coward)
PLATO
DECATUR THE GREATER
S'WONDERFUL
SKITTLES
TENDER NIPPLES (also plays Lycon)
PAILLETTE (also plays Anytus)
OOOEEE OOOEEE (also plays Meletus)
IANN EONISM

MUSICIANS

PAPA UNICORN: Piano and Synth
MOONBEAM: Trumpet and Electric Piano
SPRINKLES: Trombone and Guitar
SIMONÉ THE SHOEMAKER: Bari Sax and Tenor Sax
DEWLIP: Alto Sax
YES PLEASE: Tenor Sax
HIGH PROTEIN: Bass
HOT LAVA: Drums and Percussion

NOTES

ON CASTING: All characters may be performed by any age, gender, shape, size, ability, and ethnicity.

ON FORM/STYLE: This is a performance within a performance. All the characters in this work are Radical Fairies performing a ritual reenactment of the final hours of the life of Socrates. Although the characters of this ritual are all Radical Fairies, there is no mention of this in the spoken or sung text. The audience should never be told they are part of a Radical Fairy ritual (in a program, marketing, or a press release). That information is strictly for the collaborative team. All the audience needs to know is what they'll see and hear. The ambiguity is intentional, political, and, dare I admit, dramaturgical.

ON RECITATIVE: *The Hang* is primarily sung through. What may appear to be dialogue is recitative. **All spoken lines are in bold.**

ON SOCRATES: The Radical Fairy playing Socrates leads their performance with their Radical Fairy spirit before any traditional portrayal of Socrates.

ON PLATO: The Radical Fairy playing Plato just so happens to be philosophically against the concept of theater, which is why he was cast as Plato.

ON NAMES: The Radical Fairy names are ones chosen for the first production. As the names aren't shared with the audience, feel free to rename your own character with a name that speaks to you.

SONG LIST

SPRING

The Poison Seeps	*Musicians*
The Greeting	*Instrumental with Radical Fairies entering*
To Emote	*Radical Fairies*
The Clouds	*Socrates with Radical Fairies*
Scolding Old Codger	*S'Wonderful*
In It for the Hang	*Socrates and Radical Fairies*

SUMMER

The Ephemerals Part I	
Big Talk	*All*
Gadfly	*Skittles*
Plato's Rant	*Plato*
Aristophanes' Stand-Up	*Decatur the Greater*
Okay Boomer	*All*
Begging for the Trick	*All*
The Best Little Court Day in Years	*Socrates, High Protein*
I'm All In for the Hang	*Musicians*
Virtue	*S'Wonderful, Paillette, Iann Eonism, Simoné the Shoemaker, Radical Fairies*

FALL

The Jockey	*Oooeee Oooee with Tender Nipples, Paillette, Radical Fairies*
Harm	*Socrates, Radical Fairies*
On the One-Up	*Sprinkles*
Old Accusations	*Tender Nipples, Paillette, Radical Fairies*
Thigh to Thigh	*Socrates, Skittles, Radical Fairies*
The Package	*Skittles, Plato, Socrates, Oooeee Oooeee*
On Beauty	*Musicians*
The Ephemerals Part II	*All*

WINTER

The Poison Progresses	*Yes Please*
The Poison	*Socrates, Radical Fairies*
Aristophanes' Lament	*Decatur the Greater, Dewlip, Papa Unicorn, Sprinkles*
Only the Unknown Knows	*Tender Nipples, Socrates, Radical Fairies*
The Dirge	*Radical Fairies*
Stay a Little	*Socrates*

SPRING

Various clouds, acting like overlapping curtains, mask the playing space.

The lights fade to dark.

SONG: THE POISON SEEPS

(In the dark, the world is in turmoil from a great injustice. It mourns.

Dim light sneaks. The overlapping clouds begin to part. We are in an outdoor fecund garden of the Short Mountain sanctuary, which the performers of this ritual have made look like the insides of Socrates' body, the Universe, the Heavens, and Olympus. All at the same time.

Musicians—Papa Unicorn, Hot Lava, Yes Please, Dewlip, Moonbeam, Simoné the Shoemaker, Sprinkles, and High Protein—are spread around the world, inside trees, hung on constellations, floating amongst red blood cells.)

SONG: THE GREETING

(The actors enter. They cross the space, bow to the audience, and move to position for the start of their ritual. The actor playing Socrates steps up onto a pedestal. The other actors move into a mourning tableau. The ritual begins.)

SONG: TO EMOTE

(Radical Fairies—Tender Nipples, Skittles, S'Wonderful, Decatur the Greater, Paillette, Oooeee Oooeee, and Iann Eonism—sing, in mourning pageantry. They have dressed in their best finery/drag as a way to show up for the final moments of Socrates' life [and to outdo one another].

Socrates, dressed as a Radical Fairy version of Socrates, stands on a pedestal, having just drunk his hemlock before he entered. Is this a fever dream? We are unsure.)

RADICAL FAIRIES

Oh
Oh
Let us all weep for you.
Let us wail.

PAPA UNICORN

Let us wail.

RADICAL FAIRIES

Let us be mourners,
and beggars,
let us plead.

TENDER NIPPLES

Let us plead for Socrates.

RADICAL FAIRIES

Let us bring reckoning
to the ears.
Those who bring poison
and wreckage,
let them know.

S'WONDERFUL

In these final hours
of the life of Socrates.

RADICAL FAIRIES

Of Socrates.

SKITTLES

For if it's good enough for Socrates,
it's good enough for me.

RADICAL FAIRIES

It's good enough for me.

PAILLETTE

It's good enough for me.

(Suddenly, the Radical Fairies are in presentational bliss. As if they'd been working all year on their costumes and all month on their performances, finally getting to live their Follies *fantasy.)*

RADICAL FAIRIES

Let us all weep for you.
Let us wail.
Let us be mourners,
and beggars,
let us plead.

Let us bring reckoning
to the ears.
Those who bring poison
and wreckage,
let them know.

Let us expose our pain
and our flesh.
Let us be ugly
and pretty
so they know.

Let us fake misery
and our tears.
Let us perform what
is hopeless
to find hope.

Let us have justice here.
Let us fight.
Let us be heroes
and use e-
ve-ry means.

Let us attack and kill.
Let us free
e-ve-ry means and
every means
Socrates.

Let us have regret.
Let us weep for you.
Let us mourn for you.
Let us cry.

(The Radical Fairies become professional mourners. All trying to outdo one another.

Plato enters carrying an Ancient Greek stenograph [it's okay that they didn't exist; make it up], and is dressed very much like a stereotypical Ancient Greek. The Radical Fairies are surprised out of their mourning by Plato's entrance. Socrates watches him as Plato sets up shop in a corner where he can type. Once settled, he becomes poised to document the activities, which he will do silently throughout. Socrates waits for him to settle and then looks to us.)

SONG: THE CLOUDS

SOCRATES

Oh Athenians,
the end's the start.
My execution's done,
from being wise not smart.
Though what you're told I am
is not before you.
They spoke apparent lies
that I would bore you

with rhetoric,
with mighty words,
with heresy,
like in *The Birds* by Aristophanes.

PLATO

(Clearing his throat) **Uh-hum.**

SOCRATES

I mean,
The Toads.

PLATO

(Sighing) **Huh.**

SOCRATES

No,
not *The Toads.*
It's called *The Frogs.*

PLATO

(A passive-aggressive correction) **Hmm.**

SOCRATES

No, not *The Frogs*.
The one that pleased the crowds—
What was it—
(Trying to remember) Yes . . .
Yes . . .

PLATO

The Clouds.

SOCRATES

The Clouds.
The Clouds.

Oh Athenians,
the poison's drunk.
My drift is drifting on
and must debunk
the verdict that a thought
will trick or kill you.
Or what is worse than this?
That sleep will fill you.

From rhetoric,
from mighty words,

from heresy,
like in *The Birds*—
Clouds!
by Aristophanes.

The Clouds.
The Clouds.
The Clouds.
The Clouds.

No, not the clouds just yet.
There remains more of time
and so many questions.

Though the hours slow,
there remains still a few
to think on virtue.

And let the *clouds* be wet.
Let *them* rain so that I'm
now free to have questions.
Cease your tearful woe.
Do what clouds cannot do
and think on virtue.

No, not the clouds just yet.
There remains more of time
and so many questions.
And one apropos:
Why accusers think through
with such little virtue?

What was their plot?
Something where goats were got.
What were the means?

Something they said I taught.
I wondered,
and aloud,
if clouds weren't godly bedrock,
which led to mourning shrouds
and death by hemlock.

And death . . .

RADICAL FAIRIES

(Including musicians) And death . . .

SOCRATES

Oh Athenians,
these claims are shameless.

RADICAL FAIRIES

(Including musicians) And death . . .

SOCRATES

They say I'm eloquent
so prove me blameless.

RADICAL FAIRIES

(Including musicians) And death . . .

SOCRATES

If crimes are rhetoric,

RADICAL FAIRIES

(Including musicians) And death . . .

SOCRATES

my lone defense is
when I communicate

RADICAL FAIRIES

(Including musicians) And death . . .

SOCRATES

it's clear my sense is . . .

RADICAL FAIRIES

(Including musicians) And death . . .

SOCRATES

in the clouds,
in the clouds,
in the clouds.
In the clouds.

SONG: SCOLDING OLD CODGER

(S'Wonderful pulls Socrates into a place where the Radical Fairies all surround him in a tableau of care.)

S'WONDERFUL

Oh silly old codger,
oh silly old boy,
though the pageantry's tearful
it's all for the joy.

Oh silly professor,
has it dawned on the don,
your students are here
to help carry you on

through these
final hours
of life.

Oh contemptible scoundrel,
are you strict to the end?
Is virtue not found
in the give and the bend?

Oh daddy, oh child,
please understand,
we lovers all wish
to each hold your hand

through these
final hours
of life.

And aren't,
are-n't you done?
Haven't,
haven't you wished for someone?
To run it?
One like a son?
And take on this burden called life?

And here is,
here is the gist:
Aren't,
aren't the clouds simply mist?
They've missed you.
Missed you and wished
to take all this burden of life.

And isn't that right?
Isn't that right?

(The musicians are emphasized during an instrumental. This is their offering and we watch them as we listen.)

Oh silly old codger,
your feelings aside,
we lesser are here
to sit by your side.

We've all come to love you
and the wisest of wise
surely should know
that that is the prize

through these
final hours
of life.

And isn't that right?
Isn't that right?

(The Radical Fairies begin the wailing again. Socrates cuts it off before it becomes another "thing.")

SONG: IN IT FOR THE HANG

SOCRATES

I must insist,
if you're to stay,
that you desist
this great harangue.

For all I wish
on my final day
is to talk on virtue
and hang.

(Suddenly, the groove enters Socrates' body. We call it the kiki-cool.)

(To us) You in it to praise
or you in it for the givin'?
You in it for the craze?
You in it for the winnin'?
You in it for the bust?
You in it so they'll catch you?

To leave 'em in your dust
or you wanna be a statue?

Oh oh oh oh oh
I'm in it for the hang.

(Socrates joins the Radical Fairies.)

(To the Radical Fairies) You jonesin' for the journey brother?
You in it for the hour pop?
You doing it for God mother?
(All the glory to the power top.)
You wanna be a star sis?
You wanna be alone?
If you in it for catharsis
do you gotta break a bone?

(Socrates teaches the kiki-cool to Iann Eonism.)

Oh oh oh oh oh
I'm in it for the hang.

(Socrates and Iann Eonism have a dance together during the following verse.)

You in it for the justice?
You in it for the taste?
You in it all to trust us

'cause you wanna be erased?
You in it for the buildin'?
You in it for what's gone?
If you in it for the children
do you pass the baton?

(Socrates and Iann Eonism present the reeds who join in on the vocal chorus.)

MUSICIANS

Oh oh oh oh oh
we're in it for the hang.

(There's an instrumental while Socrates transforms the space. He is turning it into a hang, pulling out pillows, a coat rack, a bar. He makes someone a drink, hands out hors d'oeuvres, gives various Radical Fairies duties. He is grounding the space in hang reality, albeit one that still exists in this phantasmagorical environment. Iann Eonism teaches the kiki-cool to various Radical Fairies until they're all doing it. Eventually they're on board and begin taking off their mourning cloaks and reveal their party outfits underneath.)

RADICAL FAIRIES

We're in it for the action.
We're in it for the text.
We're in it for distraction.
We're in it to be next.
We're in it for the shouting.
We're in it for the quiet.
We're in it for doubting.
We're in it for the riot.

Oh oh oh oh oh
we're in it for the hang.

Oh oh oh oh oh
we're in it for the—

(The lights shift from party to contemplative.)

When the verdict is passed
and the sentence is handed,
when the jury's been rigged
and the guilty's been branded,
when the poison got ate
and it's out there gettin' plucked!

When the years are cut to days
and the days are cut to hours,
when the hours become minutes
and the relatives bring flowers,
when the poison got ate
and it's out there gettin' plucked!

When the poison got ate
and it's out there gettin' plucked.

(The Radical Fairies all focus in on one person in the audience and sing this directly to them.)

And are you a curtain?
Are you a frieze?
Where is the crack
for a Socrates?

Are you a curtain?
A body in a seat?
A shape in the dark
for us to complete?

SUMMER

SONG: THE EPHEMERALS PART I

Big Talk

(Suddenly, the ensemble are at that moment of a hang when they're energetically discussing and debating ideas, theory, relationships, and events. We bounce around from conversation to conversation. We get beginnings, middles, and ends, not necessarily in that order.

It starts with Socrates in conversation with Papa Unicorn.)

SOCRATES

And the dream said to me, cultivate and make music.

PLATO

(Stopping his typing to interrupt them and clarify Socrates)

He means philosophy, not theatrics.

SOCRATES

But then I thought, just in case dreams aren't metaphorical, let's make music.

(Papa Unicorn plays a riff and the Radical Fairies shift places.)

TENDER NIPPLES

(In conversation with Paillette) But don't you think the exchange of one fear or pleasure or pain for another fear or pleasure or pain is not the exchange of virtue?

IANN EONISM

(In conversation with Skittles) He has taken the poison, right?

SKITTLES

Haven't we all? I mean the water's up to here, gyrl.

(A conversation among S'Wonderful, Oooeee Oooeee, and Hot Lava by the drum kit.)

S'WONDERFUL

Well either way, you'll be disappointed and pleased.

OOOEEE OOOEEE

Which makes one wonder . . . The pleasure and disappointment, are they a product but beside the point?

(Hot Lava plays a riff while the ensemble changes positions, and suddenly we're in a conversation with Socrates and Plato. Plato is writing on a pad.)

SOCRATES

Could you put that down and be present with me for a moment?

(Hot Lava continues the riff and the ensemble changes positions again.)

PAILLETTE

(In conversation with Iann Eonism, Socrates, and Skittles) But my question is, do offerings constitute a hang?

IANN EONISM

You mean like bringing hummus?

SOCRATES

Or the blowing of a horn?

SKITTLES

You're filthy.

SOCRATES

You're filthy.

OOOEEE OOOEEE

(Pretending to be a gay waiter) Would you like some cream with that?

(Sprinkles on the trombone has a riff. The ensemble changes positions again.)

DECATUR THE GREATER

(In conversation with Plato) And you know they sentenced him to death for political reasons.

PLATO

And because Aristophanes sent him up in *The Clouds*.

DECATUR THE GREATER

Oh, come on, Aristophanes was a humorist. He wasn't political.

TENDER NIPPLES

(In conversation with Simoné the Shoemaker) Well I hate to put it in capitalist terms, but *I ain't buying it.*

(An exclamation of Simoné the Shoemaker while the ensemble changes positions again.)

PLATO

(In conversation with Decatur the Greater, but in a different part of the room) But when humorists give power to exaggeration, aren't they simply politicians using different tools?

(Back in the conversation with Socrates, Iann Eonism, Skittles, Oooee Oooeee, and now Tender Nipples.)

SOCRATES

My point, is in blowing, the person who blows, whom I very much doubt you took much notice of before, are they, in the eyes of their audience, suddenly made valid?

(Yes Please passes through blowing on his horn.)

TENDER NIPPLES

(To Yes Please) You're valid, baby.

SKITTLES

I'll say he's valid.

OOOEEE OOOEEE

(A euphemism, not actually offering cream) Would you like some—

SKITTLES/TENDER NIPPLES/OOOEEE OOOEEE/SOCRATES

—cream with that?

(Socrates, seeing Moonbeam, gestures for him to come into a light.)

SOCRATES

I wonder on you oh trumpet player. Do you come home early in the morning from the club, kiss your lover as they tap out the responsibility of the children?

(Moonbeam responds with a short improv.)

Are your dreamy eyes the result of a natural ease or lack of sleep?

(Moonbeam responds with a short improv.)

Or a weed of your own?

(Moonbeam responds with a short improv.)

Or the weight of a life committed to being in the musical zone?

(Moonbeam responds with a longer improv. The band kicks back into gear. The ensemble changes positions.)

PLATO

(A conversation continued with Decatur the Greater) And have you ever actually laughed at a single Aristophanes play?

DECATUR THE GREATER

Well, he's maybe not funny to our ears, but—

(The band continues and the ensemble changes positions again.)

PAILLETTE

(In conversation with Skittles and S'Wonderful) But wasn't Socrates accused of corrupting youth?

SKITTLES

(Mocking) I've been corrupted!

S'WONDERFUL

As if one doesn't go from youth to adult solely through the process of corruption.

SKITTLES

Which is a judgmental way of saying puberty.

RADICAL FAIRIES

Puberty!

SKITTLES

Puberty!

RADICAL FAIRIES

Puberty!

SOCRATES

(In conversation with Hot Lava) My assumption had always been that cum out of context is not sexy, but—

(Hot Lava plays a ba-dump-dump.)

TENDER NIPPLES

(In conversation with Paillette, S'Wonderful, and Decatur the Greater) They convicted him to death for being a non-believer.

S'WONDERFUL

Those two things, always hand in hand.

DECATUR THE GREATER

Corruption and non-believing.

S'WONDERFUL

And always so hyperbolic.

PLATO

(Interrupting) And with hyperbole comes agenda. And so we see through the accusation, or the send-up, to the tactic of attack. Rather than the truth of offense.

DECATUR THE GREATER

Aristophanes wasn't political.

PLATO

Just dated.

(Sprinkles makes an exclamation.)

S'WONDERFUL

(In conversation with Skittles) Well it seems to me the momentum is on the side of the tyrants.

SKITTLES

Because the end is nigh, gyrl.

(The reeds have a riff together as the ensemble changes positions again.)

SOCRATES

(In conversation with an audience member) I don't know the running time. I apologize to the people who like structure.
They said the hemlock would take a few moments.
But sometimes an hour. An intermissionless ninety minutes.
A day. Yours. Mine. Beyond. Perhaps we are forward while going back. Foolery reigns. Facts are in question and questions are facts. But I progress. Or acknowledge the digression of our progression. Two steps forward, one step . . .

or trip and who knows whether we are back or forward in disguise. And one deathwatch may last longer than another. Yesterday's was ninety minutes. Tonight's could be to the wee small hours. And frankly, there's something uncourageous about engaging in a mystery when you have all the proper information.

(Papa Unicorn has a riff, the ensemble changes positions again, while Plato, who was hovering by Socrates and secretly taking notes, goes to his station to write down everything Socrates said. Meanwhile, Socrates is dancing as if he's a gadfly, which irritates Paillette.)

PAILLETTE

(In conversation with Oooeee Oooeee and Tender Nipples) They sentenced him to death for being irritating.

OOOEEE OOOEEE

More for telling people they don't know what they know.

TENDER NIPPLES

It's called being a gadfly.

PAILLETTE

But aren't we suffocating in gadfly, I mean isn't everyone trying to be a gadfly now?

SKITTLES

I'm a gadfly.

PAILLETTE

(Still working the ethereal melodies) Things are changed. People make their livings being gadflies now.

(Skittles puts on a Socrates beard, roasting Socrates, and starts being that person at the party who roams around interrupting conversations with their performance.)

Gadfly

SKITTLES

I'm a gadfly.
Well somebody's gotta be.
We all can't be otters,
antelopes,
or jungle royalty.

IANN EONISM

Werk queen.

SKITTLES

I'm not the kind you find roaming
from thing to thing.
No, I'm the one who's hovering.
A gadfly hov'ring in the corner of an eye.

PAILLETTE

Nowadays to gadfly is a pastime. To be a gadfly is status.

(Skittles is playing to a different group.)

SKITTLES

Those eyes they all are goddesses
bridging the breadth
'tween little you and great big thee.

Those eyes they all use irises,
deliv'ring posts
of love and loss philosophy.

Ooh they're juicy.
Ooh their sleep attracts.
Ooh they make a gadfly want to attack.

I'm just like that gadfly hovering in the corner of an eye.

DECATUR THE GREATER

(Over by Plato, reading his text) No, Aristophanes was not responsible for the execution of Socrates.

PLATO

(Not believing her) **Mmmhmm.**

DECATUR THE GREATER

It was those other three. Whatever their names were.

PLATO

(Still writing) **Mmmhmm.**

DECATUR THE GREATER

Aristophanes was a humorist of the people.

PLATO

(Still writing) **Mmmhmm.**

DECATUR THE GREATER

Stop writing that!

(Skittles heads over to Socrates.)

SKITTLES

Woke you up this morning.
You cringed and turned away when we both chatted.
My breath exhumed.
My hair, what's left, was nested in and matted.

The feet were foul.
The pits ain't pretty.
My skin is existential.

My hygiene girl,
it ain't inconsequential.

PLATO

(Referring to Skittles) You see the problem. Once the theatrics enter, they take over—

SKITTLES

Gadfly. Gadfly.

DECATUR THE GREATER

But Aristophanes wasn't political.

PLATO

But if humor, and dated humor I might add, is used as a critique that ends up giving fodder to unconscious thinking, isn't the humor culpable for the violence that thinking inspires?

SKITTLES

The saying goes there's always one,
don't let it be you.
The saying goes there's always one—
oh well, what can you do?

Some play, some run, some devour,
and some fight.
Some troll the rainbow bridge
but some hover, dive and bite.

I'm that gadfly hovering in the corner of an eye.

I'm a gadfly.
Well somebody's gotta be.

(During the following, all the others start to gather and listen to this exchange.)

Plato's Rant

PLATO

(To Decatur the Greater) I get that you equate low-brow humor with cultural representation—

(Sarcastically) Yay populism!

—which means Aristophanes, with his phallus jokes and flatulence, is your favorite playwright. Because when he fart-jokes, you feel seen. But maybe try not to justify base humor, which leads to base behavior, like the turning of public sentiment against a philosopher because, oh yeah, it was just humor when Aristophanes made fun of him in his play, hey let's laugh at the smart kid, hey let's throw tomatoes at the thinker, hey let's get the whole mob to do it, hey let's use the mob's insecurities about not understanding things as a way to tear down any challenge to their ineptitude, hey let's find a scapegoat, hey let's kill him because everyone has confused getting what they want with virtue. But I'm here to tell you, fart jokes are not virtue. And glamour is not expression!

ALL

(A gasp) **Huh!?!**

(The Radical Fairies, so horrified by this statement, exit, vocalizing their horror all the way.)

PLATO

And poetry should be pillows to lounge on. It should be aperitif. Or . . . snacks. But we cannot allow poetry, especially the kind that's in the form of dated humor, because, yes Aristophanes is literally the most dated humorist in all of history, we cannot allow poetry to be confused with content!

(Decatur the Greater, upset, runs into the bathroom.)

SOCRATES

(To Plato, popping out from where he exited) Are you being a gadfly with an oppositional rant?

SKITTLES

(Joining Socrates in his pop-out and regarding Plato) Well somebody's gotta be.

(Meanwhile . . . in the bathroom.)

SONG: ARISTOPHANES' STAND-UP

DECATUR THE GREATER

Is virtue in a joke
that's dated?
Is virtue in a joke,
then hated?
When the past howls,
but the present doesn't get it,
is the virtue stale?
Then the virtue shucked
'cause the present thinks it sucked?
Is virtue only alive and drinking it in?
Or are you just angry when you don't fit in?

Is virtue only found in things that last?
If so then you and I don't stand a chance.

Is virtue in the pop
ref'rence?
Is virtue in the pop
deference?
When the past howls
but the present doesn't get it

is the virtue stale?
Is the work then bloated
when the reference is footnoted?
Is virtue only alive? Should we regret it?
Or are you just angry that you still don't get it?

Is virtue only found in things that last?
If so then you and I don't stand a chance.

Oh but the dead are dead and gone.
And the living matter more.
But a joke's a little con,
like romance:
Seduce you,
please you,
leave you
waiting for
more virtue.

Is virtue only found in things that last?
If so then you and I don't stand a chance.

(The Radical Fairies enter wearing beards, in the guise of Socrates. It's a group of people having fun with a dated pop culture reference and finding virtue in the consideration of it.)

SONG: OKAY BOOMER

ALL

Okay Boomer.
Okay hon.
Okay flapper,
ain't your flappin' done?
Okay Greatest,
you're the peak.

Okay White Man
and Ancient Greek.

Okay!
Hey!
Whatever!

Okay Boomer.
Okay Y.
Okay Grandpa,
you were once a G.I.,
woo!
Okay X,
You Slacker freak.
Okay White Man
and Ancient Greek.

Okay!
Hey!
Whatever!

When the alphabet is over
get your Z Z Z Z Zs.
Then
you can free yourself
of
a
Socrates.
Okay Lincoln,
"Four score" and forefather.
Okay Jesus—
I mean Jesus!
Why bother?
Okay, you who can't
keep your wooden teeth in.

Okay Boomer
And Elizabeth(i)n.

(During the following, the Radical Fairies, one at a time, take off their beards and throw them in a fire pit.)

Okay, OK!
Okay, OK!
Okay, OK!
Okay, OK!
Okay, OK!
Okay, OK!
Okay, OK!
Okay, OK!

(Tender Nipples lights the pit on fire.)

RADICAL FAIRIES

Hey!

Okay Silent,
you wouldn't speak.
Okay Y-ner,
shut yer beak!
Okay Greatest!
Whoa-kay freak!
Okay Boomer
and Ancient Greek!

SONG: BEGGING FOR THE TRICK

(The Radical Fairies all celebrate their performance. Iann Eonism interrupts them.)

IANN EONISM

(An idea, to us) Trial! Do your trial.
(To Socrates) Trial! Do your trial.

SOCRATES

(Feigning that he doesn't know what they're talking about)
Oh no, I couldn't possibly.

ALL

Trial! Do your trial.

PAILLETTE

Even Socrates got a party trick.

ALL

Trial! Do your trial!

SOCRATES

(Feigning being ill) Oh but the poison, oh how I'm sick.
(A fake cough) Uh-huh.

ALL

Trial! Do your trial.

PAILLETTE

Even Socrates got a party trick.

RADICAL FAIRIES

Tell us all where we have been
so we know where we are at.
Limerick all the legalese.
Dandy up the tit for tat.
Pretty pretty pretty please
do the trial of Socrates.
Tell the tale how you devoured;

how every argument's deflowered
And TELL IT
IN YOUR BEST
NOËL COWARD!

SOCRATES

If you insist—

IANN EONISM

(An aside to Plato) He can't resist the Coward
when he's pissed.

SKITTLES

It's his shtick.

PAILLETTE

'Cause even Socrates got a party trick.

SONG: THE BEST LITTLE COURT DAY IN YEARS

(Performed to a medium tempo walking bassline.)

NOËL COWARD

(Played by Socrates) Oh, how I wish you were there.
The court was full cram.
It was gam next to gam
and the sweat left a scent of arousal.
For the heat of debate
made us pontificate
on the men as opposed to the spousal.
It was gayer than Spartans
or panty-less tartans
spinning in peacock parade.
For to add to the fever,
of incitement sans beaver,

the house had been stacked with the trade.
Our dear little mentor
got each little rent whore
to pack the top balcony tiers.
Oh what a show,
don't you know,
'twas the best little court day in years.

Oh how I wish you were there.
For the prudes on the panel
were all dudes wearing flannel—
no just kidding we'll keep it in period.
They wore last year's sad sandals
as if those weren't the scandals
and tried to defend their myriad
of performative blame.
Oh is there no shame
to this triumphant triumvirate trio,
whose bland little test
was a litmus at best,
just a list not panache for a row.
They were Meletus, Anytus, and Lycon.

(The Triumvirate [Meletus/Anytus/Lycon played by Oooeee Oooeee, Paillette, and Tender Nipples] are revealed in the hollow of a tree/kidney. We just see their faces/headpieces, so the actors don't have to change costumes entirely just yet.

Almost as soon as they appear, Noël Coward shuts the window on the tree hollow/kidney and they disappear.)

Not a single one destined for icon
status. Still we're sniffing the rears
for their show
don't you know,
'twas the best little court day in years.

Oh how I wish you were there.
For our grand Master Gadfly
deconstructed the tad lie
the trio had used and fermented.
He humiliated
and decapitated
each charge that each had invented.
For the three prosecutors
all had sons who were suitors
of him, some might call them "mentees."
So you know the corruption
they charged was eruption
of the member of stiff Socrates.
Oh yes it was clear
he was tried for his queer
appetites and not what they said.
For he'd slept with the son
of, well at least one,
and encouraged the others to bed
who they would.
Oh what a show,
don't you know
'twas the best little court day that could.

'Twas a day for the ages,
which I'm sure they'll write pages
and lectures about.
The stern prosecution
with their thin execution
revealed not a doubt
their affair had been jumbled.
Still how I was humbled
to hear it proclaimed
that our kind little muskrat
was found guilty of that

tired task of inciting the tamed.
With the verdict decided
before court subsided,
and not from a jury of peers,
'twas all just a show,
don't you know,
but the best little court day in years.

(The Radical Fairies cheer the trick.)

SONG: I'M ALL IN FOR THE HANG

(Papa Unicorn counts us in. Socrates joins in on the count and encourages the musicians to take over the space. They do. The Radical Fairies sit back and enjoy. At some point in the song, S'Wonderful and Paillette get an idea to do a number and grab Simoné the Shoemaker to join them. Oooeee Oooeee meanwhile decides to change costumes into their Meletus outfit [in a corner of the room and not stealing attention].)

SONG: VIRTUE

(S'Wonderful and Paillette come into the space with Simoné the Shoemaker. Meanwhile, Oooeee Oooeee gestures to Tender Nipples to join in changing costumes. He also does so discreetly.)

S'WONDERFUL/PAILLETTE

Yeah, yeah, yeah, yeah, yeah, yeah, yeah!

RADICAL FAIRIES/MUSICIANS

Yeah, yeah, yeah, yeah, yeah, yeah, yeah!

S'WONDERFUL/PAILLETTE

Yeah, yeah, yeah, yeah, yeah, yeah, yeah!

RADICAL FAIRIES/MUSICIANS
Yeah, yeah, yeah, yeah, yeah, yeah, yeah!

S'WONDERFUL/PAILLETTE
What do you mean by virtue?
What do you mean by good?
What do you mean by virtue?
What do you mean—

RADICAL FAIRIES
Oh just get it!

(Simoné the Shoemaker has a sax solo.)

S'WONDERFUL/PAILLETTE
Yeah, yeah, yeah, yeah, yeah, yeah, yeah!

RADICAL FAIRIES/MUSICIANS
Yeah, yeah, yeah, yeah, yeah, yeah, yeah!

S'WONDERFUL/PAILLETTE
Yeah, yeah, yeah, yeah, yeah, yeah, yeah!

RADICAL FAIRIES/MUSICIANS
Yeah, yeah, yeah, yeah, yeah, yeah, yeah!

S'WONDERFUL/PAILLETTE
What do you mean by virtue?
What do you mean by good?
What do you mean by virtue?
What do you mean—

RADICAL FAIRIES
Oh just get it!

(S'Wonderful has a scat solo.)

S'WONDERFUL/PAILLETTE

Yeah, yeah, yeah, yeah, yeah, yeah, yeah!

RADICAL FAIRIES/MUSICIANS

Yeah, yeah, yeah, yeah, yeah, yeah, yeah!

S'WONDERFUL/PAILLETTE

Yeah, yeah, yeah, yeah, yeah, yeah, yeah!

RADICAL FAIRIES/MUSICIANS

Yeah, yeah, yeah, yeah, yeah, yeah, yeah!

S'WONDERFUL/PAILLETTE

What do you mean by virtue?
What do you mean by good?
What do you mean by virtue?
What do you mean—

RADICAL FAIRIES

Oh just get it!

(Paillette has a scat solo.)

S'WONDERFUL/PAILLETTE

Yeah, yeah, yeah, yeah, yeah, yeah, yeah!

RADICAL FAIRIES/MUSICIANS

Yeah, yeah, yeah, yeah, yeah, yeah, yeah!

S'WONDERFUL/PAILLETTE

Yeah, yeah, yeah, yeah, yeah, yeah, yeah!

RADICAL FAIRIES/MUSICIANS

Yeah, yeah, yeah, yeah, yeah, yeah, yeah!

S'WONDERFUL/PAILLETTE

What do you mean by virtue?
What do you mean by good?
What do you mean by virtue?
What do you mean—

RADICAL FAIRIES

Oh just get it!

(Tender Nipples beckons for Paillette to join in changing costumes, and they do [also discreetly]. Meanwhile, Iann Eonism has a dance solo.)

S'WONDERFUL/IANN EONISM

Yeah, yeah, yeah, yeah, yeah, yeah, yeah!

RADICAL FAIRIES/MUSICIANS

Yeah, yeah, yeah, yeah, yeah, yeah, yeah!

(S'Wonderful and Iann Eonism get the idea to get Socrates involved, and the other Radical Fairies gather around him to hear what he thinks virtue is.)

S'WONDERFUL/IANN EONISM

Yeah, yeah, yeah, yeah, yeah, yeah, yeah!

RADICAL FAIRIES/MUSICIANS

Yeah, yeah, yeah, yeah, yeah, yeah, yeah!

RADICAL FAIRIES

What do you mean by virtue?
What do you mean by good?
What do you mean by virtue?
What do you mean—Oh just get it!

(As the party is just about to peak . . .)

FALL

There is a crash. The Triumvirate emerge out of a tree/artery direct from the underworld.

SONG: THE JOCKEY

MELETUS

The party is over.
The hemlock is plucked.
The parent is early
and now you're all fucked.

RADICAL FAIRIES

The party is over.
The hemlock is plucked.
The parent is early
and now we're all fucked.

TRIUMVIRATE/RADICAL FAIRIES

The party is over.
The hemlock is plucked.
The parent is early
and now we're all fucked.

MELETUS

So run little children.
Flush all the drugs.
Leave half-drunk booze
in collectible mugs.

TRIUMVIRATE

So run little children.
Swallow or spit.
You wanted the best
but are left with the bit.

MELETUS

Who got the bit?
Who got the bit?
Who got the bit in their mouth now?
Who got the bit?
Who got the bit?
Who stuck with the ball
and the stream of their spit?
Drip,
drip.

TRIUMVIRATE

Oh shit!

MELETUS

Betcha didn't think,
'cause you never never think

no never no no,
someone like me is the Jockey.

TRIUMVIRATE

Oh shit!

MELETUS

Betcha didn't think,
'cause you never never think no never no no.

TRIUMVIRATE

Someone like me is the Jockey!

MELETUS

Caligula is gonna ride ya.
Leopold will genocide ya.
Pisistratus pin your hide just—

TRIUMVIRATE

like you're a donkey.

MELETUS

Who got the bit?
Who got the bit?
Who got the bit in their mouth now?
Who got the bit?
Who got the bit?
Who stuck with the ball
and the stream of their spit?
Drip,
drip.

TRIUMVIRATE

Oh shit!

MELETUS

Betcha didn't think,
'cause you never never think no never no no,
someone like me is the Jockey.

TRIUMVIRATE

Oh shit!

MELETUS

Betcha didn't think,
'cause you never never think no never no no.

TRIUMVIRATE

Someone like me is the Jockey!

MELETUS

Enver Pasha pick a part ya.
Tokugawa queen of heart ya.
Cromwell gonna clause and god ya.
And Porfirio Diaz ya.
Ivan gonna Novgorod ya.
Stalin kills and writes a rondle.
Mitch McConnell gonna fondle—

TRIUMVIRATE

your private sector.

MELETUS

Genghis Khan will penetrate ya.
Andrew Jackson starve and gate ya.
Fu Sheng gonna void and beat ya.
Jabberwocky gonna eat ya.

TRIUMVIRATE

Jabberwocky gonna eat ya.
Jabberwocky gonna eat ya.

(The Radical Fairies are all mesmerized by the Triumvirate and begin to join them until Socrates is alone.)

Your goose is cooked.
Your king got rooked.
Whatcha gonna do when your venue booked
your death,
your death,
your death?

Your goose is cooked.
Your king got rooked.
Whatcha gonna do when your venue booked
your death,
your death,
your death?

MELETUS

But I ain't no Mitch McConnell.
And I ain't no Pisistratus.
No, I ain't no Jabberwocky.
(To Socrates) I'm the one who used your talkie-talkie
to end you.

(Lycon and Anytus put Socrates in the corner.)

The party is over.
The hemlock is plucked.
You cuss my name
go on and cuss.

MUSICIANS	RADICAL FAIRIES
The party is over.	The party is over.
The hemlock is plucked.	The hemlock is plucked.
Meletus, Meletus,	Meletus, Meletus,
Meletus	Meletus

ALL	MELETUS
The party is over.	Go on and cuss
The hemlock is plucked.	my name.
Meletus, Meletus, Meletus.	I hold the reins.

SONG: HARM

(The Radical Fairies now all form a choir in opposition to Socrates.)

RADICAL FAIRIES

And didn't Meletus say you harm us,
you harm us,
you harm us?
And didn't you then ask,
"But who then improves us?"
Improves us?
And didn't Meletus say,
"The laws do improve us"?
Improve us.

And didn't you then ask,
"But who Meletus? Who then?
Not what but who then improves us?"
Improves us?
And didn't Meletus say,
"The judges
improve us"?
And didn't you then ask,
"Who else then
improves us?"
And didn't Meletus say,
"The senators improve us"?
And didn't you then say,

"Who else then? Oh tell us!"?
And didn't Meletus say,
that all men improve us,
except
you?

SOCRATES

Does one man do harm
and all else good?
Is this what the law enforces?
Or is it not true
that the many will ride
but the stableman cares for the horses?

And if a lone man
corrupts the young,
is this not called faulty labors?
For then the corruptor regrets to have
the corrupted as his neighbors.

RADICAL FAIRIES

But didn't Meletus say that you don't
believe, plus—
believe, plus—
And didn't he then claim,
"An atheist's among us"?
Among us?
And didn't Meletus say
that you don't believe God?
Believe God.
And didn't you then ask,

"But who Meletus, who won't
believe a moon or
a sun in

the sky there?"
And didn't Meletus say,
"It's you won't."
It's you won't.
And didn't he then state,
"You say they're
just stones there"?
And didn't you then say,
"When poets write I say things,
like Aristophanes,
they're using a license,
we call it poetic"?
And didn't Meletus swear that,
"You swear by nothing,
except you"?

SOCRATES

Did ever a man who sees a stable
then not believe in horses?
Did ever a man believe in man
and not think what the source is?

Did ever a man who believes in wealth
deny the proof of classes?
Did ever a man who believes in mules
then not believe in asses?

(Socrates taps Sprinkles into the debate the way you would a wrestler.)

SONG: ON THE ONE-UP

(Sprinkles, on trombone, plays his thoughts on one-upping.)

SONG: OLD ACCUSATIONS

(Tender Nipples, Paillette, and Oooeee Oooeee take off their Triumvirate outfits and are themselves again.)

TENDER NIPPLES

An old accusation's
heavy.
It's had the years to hide.
It's had the years to grow and mold on bone.

PAILLETTE

An old accusation's
steady.
It's had the years to slide
inside a thought and sew itself to stone.

TENDER NIPPLES

An old accusation rates your studies of Heaven
and all the Earth's laws.
An old accusation states you've argued the worse is
the much better cause.

PAILLETTE

An old accusation turns the questions to demons
just under the beds.
A young listener then learns an old man is leering
in woods and in heads.
Al-
ways
in
the
heads.

TENDER NIPPLES/PAILLETTE
To defend from what's lore is
like fighting a cloud, for
the accuser will score by
hiding in crowds. Or
an old accusation, when it's
bold and assured,
is too much inured to
ever be cured.

TENDER NIPPLES
An old accusation claims young minds were infested
with too many views.

PAILLETTE
An old accusation frames young hearts were molested
and love was confused.

TENDER NIPPLES
An old accusation shows their faults reflected
as they are anointed.

PAILLETTE
As old accusations flow, one finger's selected
and three fingers pointed
right
back
at
yourself.

TENDER NIPPLES/PAILLETTE
To defend from what's new
is so simple and clear.
You begin with what's true
in the front not the rear.

But old accusations are
a messier lot;
their teaching's been taught
and tied in a knot.

With old accusations rating
the studies of Heaven
and all the Earth's laws.
With old accusations stating:
we've argued the worse
is the much better cause.

(The Radical Fairies join them, except Skittles, who sheepishly approaches Socrates, trying to get on his good side again.)

RADICAL FAIRIES

With old accusations swearing:
with new thoughts we soil
the old use of the red herring
that truth has been foiled.
With old accusations saying
doubts are diseases.
An old accusation braying
Socrates teases
you all
to create a cabal,
to make sun and moon fall.
Could we really be
all
that
bad?

(The Radical Fairies gesture to Socrates and Skittles, who have struck a love pose, as if to suggest the horrible/bad thing Socrates was accused of is hooking up.

Skittles puts his hand on Socrates' thigh. Socrates sees the audience watching and takes Skittles' hand off his thigh and puts it on Skittles'.)

SONG: THIGH TO THIGH

SOCRATES

Thigh to thigh here satyr,
hanging 'midst
(Gesturing to the audience)
the company.

SKITTLES

Gotta make it subtle
so we make it sweet.

SOCRATES

How easy would it be though . . .

SOCRATES/SKITTLES

To lean a little deeper,
wrap limbs and tongues and gazes?

SOCRATES

But you really aren't a keeper,
for I've not the heart for phases.

(Skittles inches his hand back to Socrates' thigh. He has a whistle solo as a seduction.)

Sigh to sigh now satyr,
flirting makes the hang grow sweeter.

(S'Wonderful and Paillette saunter by, gossiping about Socrates and Skittles.)

SKITTLES

Friends, with knowing smirks,
saunter by to witness—

SOCRATES/SKITTLES

the private swagger method.

And will we won't we best
the rules of an affection;
so give permission for the rest
to have a cheater's imperfection?

(Socrates moves away from Skittles.)

SOCRATES

Yes, I've got a wife who is a husband,
a crush who is a flow to ebb,
I give my daily offering
to the chronic
and bubonic platonic web.

And you've a mentor off in England,
another one in Tennessee,
you play the Penny Arcade
then eat peaches
from the Teaches of the Peaches tree.

(Skittles moves their hand to Socrates' crotch [under his outfit].)

You pop your mothers like they're mints,
your heroes like you're jonesing for 'em,
you jump from daddy to daddy
and queen to queen;
from Bond to Bourne to the Ru alum.

You pop your mothers like they're mints,
your heroes like it's all carefree,
you jump from daddy to daddy
and boy to boy,
from girl to gyrl and even me.

Still I'll take the tension in the bell chime of you,
though it leaves you with a lifetime of revue.

My oh my dear satyr,
queerness needs its time and place.

SOCRATES/SKITTLES

Not due to the dictates
but authenticity.
How easy would it be though . . .

SOCRATES

To let you please this geezer?
Wrap limbs and tongues and biting
and win the title of appeaser?
If it weren't that Plato's writing.

(Plato stops typing.)

PLATO

Sorry.

SONG: THE PACKAGE

OOOEEE OOOEEE

(Looking at what Plato is writing) You left out the part where they gazed into each other's eyes.

PLATO

Because romanticism, and poetry, and yes, aesthetics have a way of blinding—

SKITTLES

You're telling me the package isn't also the content? I mean for sure I'm carving a place in the world for my fabulous. I mean gyrl, you might as well be wearing a black T-shirt from the H&M at the queer anti-capitalist march.

PLATO

What?

SKITTLES

Oh this queer pride where they had an alternative march where the organizers told all the anarchists to wear the black colors for a unified look and to take out the frills of the corporate pride. And so what do the anarchists do?

They show up, tens of thousands of them, wearing black jeans and T-shirts to protest corporations. Except where do you purchase a black T-shirt? From a corporation. And sure they'd printed the slogans saying the anti-things blazing across those T-shirts, but if you're asking me, from a distance a slogan and an advertisement look awfully similar. I mean, I was the only one in a queer activist march roller-skating about in a handmade gold lamé hot-pant. As if the sensible black was saying anything other than, the wanker heterosexuals are making you take yourself too seriously. And let me tell you, that's the sort of thing makes you want to drink Coca-Cola on a Mack truck with a bunch of go-go boys.

SOCRATES

Are you being a gadfly by using an oppositional rant . . . as foreplay?

SKITTLES

(Flirting, back to his gadfly melody) Well somebody's gotta be.

SONG: ON BEAUTY

(Socrates and Skittles look back into each other's eyes but suddenly the poison begins to affect Socrates. He sees clouds. All else disappears for him, and he begins to make his way to the clouds. Skittles, Tender Nipples, and Iann Eonism rush to bring Socrates back to earth. Suddenly, the clouds envelope everyone and they become intoxicated.)

SONG: THE EPHEMERALS PART II

(As they succumb to intoxication the space changes; it breathes. A giant heart/lotus leaf appears and the ensemble all find their way to it. They are at the point in the hang where everyone is lounging on one another.

This time, while high, they are trying to have deep conversation. Some more successfully than others. The Radical Fairies are focused on whoever is singing or soloing during the following.)

DECATUR THE GREATER

During the Egyptian theater, everyone was high. The performers, the audience: high. And when it came time for the human sacrifice in the story—

PAILLETTE

Because there is always a human sacrifice—

DECATUR THE GREATER

They would actually kill someone.

TENDER NIPPLES

So feel free to partake in the hemlock of your choosing.

OOOEEE OOOEEE

(Meaning "oh I did") Gyrl.

TENDER NIPPLES

Gatherings are always more fun when everyone's risking the adventure together.

OOOEEE OOOEEE

I hope that's not true.

(Socrates stands, and the Radical Fairies and musicians all grab a piece of his outfit. It transforms to envelop them all.)

PAILLETTE

But suicide is or is not a sin?

SOCRATES

Well, I understand there's a collective dirty secret that man's a prisoner who has no right to run away but—

DECATUR THE GREATER

(Not aware that she's singing her inner thoughts aloud) Everyone liked Socrates in *The Clouds* when it was performed the first time.

S'WONDERFUL

These have to be his final moments. Even when they're only at mid-point, one feels an ending. I said that so confidently, but I'm not sure it's true.

OOOEEE OOOEEE

It could be indigestion or impatience or—

S'WONDERFUL
Indulgence manifesting as sentimental manipulation—

DECATUR THE GREATER
Everyone laughed and Socrates stood up in the audience and waved the first time.

TENDER NIPPLES
Well, if there's one thing I know, mixed company does not like the extremity of a happy ending.

DECATUR THE GREATER
It's not Aristophanes' fault they took it too seriously when they revived it.

SOCRATES
Platoooooo.

RADICAL FAIRIES
Platoooooo.

SOCRATES
Put down that device.

SKITTLES
Yeah, put down your device, Plato.

OOOEEE OOOEEE
Would you like some cream with that—

DECATUR THE GREATER
It's not Aristophanes' fault they used his work against our Socrates.

SOCRATES

(To Plato) I'm simply saying, this writing you do is making my philosophical practice a manual for middle management, which removes our togetherness by setting the thought and exchange outside of ourselves, on a device.

SKITTLES

Plato is the person who, at a dinner party—

ALL BUT PLATO

Pulls out their phone.

S'WONDERFUL

Be nice to my Plato.

ALL BUT PLATO

(Pulling Plato down amongst them) Platoooooo.

DECATUR THE GREATER

They used his work against his friend.

SOCRATES

(To Plato) But let's get one thing clear regarding our time together. Something we all have in common is we ask people to validate their existence via our ability to relate to them. And so far,

you haven't proven
yourself
relatable.

So far,
you haven't proven
yourself
relatable.

So far. You haven't. You haven't.

ALL BUT PLATO

(To the audience) So far,
you haven't proven
yourself
relatable.

So far,
you haven't proven
yourself
relatable.

So far. You haven't. You haven't.

DECATUR THE GREATER

It's not Aristophanes' fault they used his humor to attack and kill.

SOCRATES

(To the audience) What you have offered is your presence. Thank you, but more than presence is required. Creation is a—

ALL BUT PLATO

Group effort.

OOOEEE OOOEEE

Would you like some cream with that—

DECATUR THE GREATER

It's not Aristophanes' fault the status quo are vile. It's not always the radical thinkers' fault the normative are vile. It's not any of our faults. It's not. It's not. It's noooooot.

WINTER

SONG: THE POISON PROGRESSES

(Yes Please on tenor sax calls out the progress of the poison. Socrates suddenly gets sick. He gestures for the space to be cleared. He needs room to breathe. Skittles and S'Wonderful go to Socrates to help him. Tender Nipples runs to get something for Socrates to puke in. Paillette prays. Oooeee Oooeee starts to get the dry heaves from seeing Socrates getting them. Decatur the Greater can't deal and starts weeping in a corner. Plato starts writing everything down again.)

SONG: THE POISON

(Socrates begins walking it off. The Radical Fairies take on aspects of the poison. He's in a full-on fever dream now.)

SOCRATES

Beware the aesthetic of the New Age guru.
Beware the seductive ease of the seller's breakthrough.
Beware the rush you get from troubles, when they're spoken.

Beware the fear of the sexual practice.
Beware the disgust you feel from the mad and tactless.
Beware the smell you spray to block out all that's broken.

Beware the commerce of your outrage:
the act of courage on the stage
of streets and phones and socials we all soak in.

Beware girl,
the poison.

Take a broomstick and ride it like
a witch or horse or a pauper's bike.
And then go to every corner that is taken.

Squat or spread or cuddle up.
Nothing's owned, what's down is up.
What's up is down, especi'lly in the break-in.

But when the tyranny keeps stepping first,
'cause the first is last has been reversed,
you'll know the woke ain't woke if they ain't wakin'.

Beware girl, the poison.

RADICAL FAIRIES

You'll dance and shower in the streets
when all is won.
The platitudes and adjectives
will all be flung.

Like darts that miss their mark,
they'll shoot right past the staff,
and the sloshing cheers
will put the poison
into every glass.

SOCRATES

Beware the person with the time
to make their point with perfect rhyme;
they're sitting in the lap of occupation.

Beware the working little bee
who wants to tell you what to see;
he'll kill himself to prove an allegation.

Beware the victim who just complains;
they never really want the change
and often were the one who screwed the nation.

Beware girl,
the poison.

(Socrates and the Radical Fairies create a tableau of resignation.)

SONG: ARISTOPHANES' LAMENT

DECATUR THE GREATER

Mistakes are made,
'cause judgments come
like mornings,
when eyelids and your arms don't ease the light.

Colors displayed.
The oranges glow
in mornings.

The yellows nag until it's all too bright.

And the days you want
aren't the days you have.
And more
the sun won't change.

So you're nonchalant
'bout the days you have.
And still
the sun won't change.

So you'll pick a target,
flesh and bone like you,
and burn it through.

Mistakes are made,
and judgments come
like mornings,
when eyelids and your arms won't ease the sun.

(The Radical Fairies change Socrates into a burial dress.)

SONG: ONLY THE UNKNOWN KNOWS

(Socrates is ready for his final resting place.)

TENDER NIPPLES

Only the unknown knows.

SOCRATES

You may think you know, but you may not know what you think you know.

TENDER NIPPLES

For only the unknown knows.
That's how the praying goes.
When life is daunting and one is wanting,
one has to presuppose,
only the unknown knows.

SOCRATES/TENDER NIPPLES

Are only the gods then true?
Do they know but we pursue?
No disrespect meant,
our intellect meant we never really knew.
Wond'ring is all we do.

ALL

But what a wondrous thing, to wonder.
Wondering is praying.
Wondering is holy.
Holy gods.

TENDER NIPPLES

Only the unknown knows.
That's what our writing shows.
All our declaring, questions and sharing
is a collective prose,
That only the unknown knows.

SOCRATES/TENDER NIPPLES

Are only the gods then true?
For they have the better view.
Not just above us but inside and of us.
Is our job to think it through?
Wond'ring, not seeing true?

ALL

But what a wondrous thing to wonder.
Wondering is praying.
Wondering is holy.
Holy gods.

How can you not know this?
How can the heavens spin
and you call it sin
to wonder?

TENDER NIPPLES

Humans who say they're right
know they've not seen the light.
But humans who don't know how their own plot goes
by their attempting might
come up with some insight
to wonder.

RADICAL FAIRIES

To wonder.
To wonder.

PLATO

(Reading what he has just written) **He was beginning to grow cold about the groin, when he uncovered his face, for he had covered himself up, and said—they were his last words:**

SOCRATES

(Exiting to the side but still in the space) **Crito, I owe a cock to Asclepius; will you remember to pay the debt?**

PLATO

"The debt shall be paid," said Crito. "Is there anything else?" There was no answer to this question; but in a

minute or two a movement was heard, and the attendants uncovered him; his eyes were set, and Crito closed his eyes and mouth. Such was the end.

SONG: THE DIRGE

(The ensemble create a second-line funeral dirge for Socrates. The following is performed in a continuous vocal round.)

RADICAL FAIRIES (FIRST GROUP)

Hear ye, hear ye!
The beauty, will it queer ye?
The state has argued
and the hemlock seeps.
Should this injustice lead us to weep or peep?

RADICAL FAIRIES (SECOND GROUP)

I'm a gadfly.

RADICAL FAIRIES (THIRD GROUP)

Beware girl,
the poison.
The poison.

PAPA UNICORN

(Improvisational singing using any of these lines)
Let us all weep for you!
Let us wail!
Let us be mourners
and beggars.
Let us plead.

Let us be frivolous
and exhaust

all of our humor
and anger
in our sweat.

Let us expose our pain
and our flesh.
Let us be ugly
and pretty,
so they know.

Let us be free of you.
Let us grow.
Let us inherit
and further.
Let us go.

(The round ends with the ensemble all singing as they exit.)

RADICAL FAIRIES

Let us think of you.
Let us think *with* you.
Let us *be* with you.
Through our lives.

(All that remains is Plato typing and Socrates off to the side.)

SOCRATES

Was the depiction accurate?

PLATO

It's not what I've documented.

SOCRATES

You've edited . . .

PLATO

The embellishment of others. So that it may be clear. And not used against you.

SOCRATES

Thank you. There is, I wonder, perhaps too much fluidity in telling.

PLATO

So you agree, it was good that I have written it down.

SOCRATES

I have suspicions to the contrary, but I don't wish to confuse suspicion with wondering. And I would so prefer we wonder together rather than be in . . . suspicion.

PLATO

But it has finished.

SOCRATES

Should I leave?

PLATO

(Looking at his notes) **It says your feet have grown cold.**

SOCRATES

(Meaning, they're fine) **Hmm.**

PLATO

(Reading) **And it says, "Such was the end, of our friend; concerning whom I may truly say, that of all the men of his time whom I have known, he was the wisest and justest and best."**

SOCRATES

Am I to be a statue then? Fixed and knowing. And finished?

SONG: STAY A LITTLE

SOCRATES

Have we matured enough to wear the robes and silk?
And all their similar ilk?
The panic of malaise, the boredom and the craze of sighs,
the rolling doldrum eyes,
when cheeks lose their rose?

Are we all prone to prattle on to win the prize?
To ease the weight of the skies?
And fill the space that lacks the pace of pomp and circumstance
with random beauty dance?
Will we muse or pose?

Before we're committed to end all our wit
with plagues of opinions,
please linger some longer, consider the stronger
who are but the minions
of thinking on virtue.

Or am I a fool?
I could be a fool.

There remains more of time
to sit for a bit
languishing in a fancy.

Though we've dwindled our lives,
adrift as we sift,
we'll waste more if antsy.

So come near me again
before I'm a goner.
Reflect upon honor and love.

And come argue again,
before we are settled,
before we will let ourselves know.

Please make me long and regret,
within a final breath.

Come blush with this fool.
Blush with me.

(The lights fade to black.

After the curtain call, the audience, cast, crew, and musicians may stay and jam for as long as the spontaneity seduces.)